Other titles
by
Corey Hamilton

Keep Left
Exit Is A Safe Place
No One Shall Be Spared
Open Up
Mash Notes
Mash Notes: vol 2
Too Personal
Lonely Night Songs
2 Days
Unhyped
Time Marches On
Thirty Three
VI
What If?
Magic Bus
How I Remember It
Cease & Desist
Sensible Shoes
Do Not Ever Have Any Good Ideas
DNA
I Am NOT With The Band
Wedge Politics
My Side Project

Society s Grip

Copyright © 1999 Corey Hamilton

All rights reserved. No part of this book may be reproduced or transmitted in any form or by any means, graphic, electronic or mechanical, including photocopying and recording, or by any information storage or retrieval system without written permission from the publisher, except for brief passages quoted in a review.

Hamilton, Corey
      Society's Grip/Corey Hamilton

Poems, prose.

ISBN 978-0-9697305-6-9

Back cover photography by Kelli Ferrigan © 1992
Front cover illustration by Corey Hamilton © 1991
Design/Layout by Corey Hamilton

Second Printing

Published by Dramatic Situations
          P.O. Box 696
          Edmonton, AB
          T5J 2L4
          CANADA
www.dramaticsituations.com

Text printed on 100% post consumer recycled FSC-certified paper.

Society s Grip

Corey Hamilton

R.I.P.

And then, of course, there are those who shrink from all contact with simple people, and the tactless jokesters who talk down to them---they succeed in only in making the poor souls more sharply aware than ever of their presumption. I know that we human beings were not created equal and can not be, but I am of the opinion that he who keeps aloof from the so-called rabble in order to preserve the respect he feels he is due is just as reprehensible as the coward who hides from his enemies because he fears to be defeated by them.

-Goethe-

#344

SARAH
(SOCIETY'S GRIP)
-EPILOGUE-

In the beginning. In the beginning there was nothing. I was nothing. And I think I am still nothing.

I needed something to take me from nowhere to somewhere. A split of a split second. I want to grasp to hold and to burn down. And up. In order for my grammar to be understood all who scan (nobody reads paper anymore; it's meant to be scorned and then burned) you must fall. Fall down and up and back down. Slammed hard. Proofreading is not necessary. Rereading is not necessary. Take it or leave. Leave it. And leave me running down. It means about the same to me as I was in the beginning.

Concrete. I need concrete to build something that was real. To be awake and build. My family moans its disbelief as they chase my chicken thoughts away. They are not concrete. They are profit. They are not real. They are clouds above the soil and blood. I need the soil and blood to make my concrete. The strongest foundations are made of this. The foundations and fortifications are one perforation in my scars. Minute. Minute families have left a void without my consultation. Indeed. They will not be in my foundations. My environment is now at my, in the beginning.

Wire must be found. Wire is just as important in my basement as the concrete. Project. The wire makes my concrete flexible. Project basement. Protect my flexibility and I will in turn protect project basement's flexibility. Turn and twist on my student funding. The wire has sifted out all the bad sports. The wire keeps the arts. Arts. Arts feel like meat. Tender and there. Tasteful and disgusting. Think what went into meat. Think what went into arts. Think what went into wire. Meat, arts, wire. What went into them disgusts most civilians. Meat onto arts into wire through me. My kingdom for wire. There is too much danger in my head to melt meat into arts. This can not happen. Wire prevents this. It has identical beginnings and endings. You can't tell which is which. That's what makes my in the beginning special. No one will be able to tell if it's in the ending or in the beginning. In my in the ending or in my in the beginning.

Wood. Dead or alive. It's natural. Being natural is important. Like laughter or crying or anger. This makes no sense? Three byproducts can't mix:

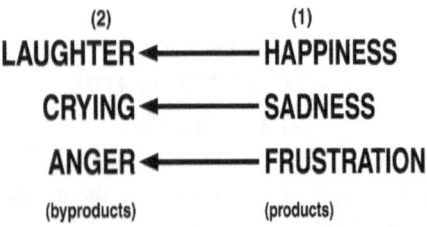

Talk amongst yourselves about this. And I think you'll agree. Of course you can mix them all. It's natural. Natural products, natural mixes:

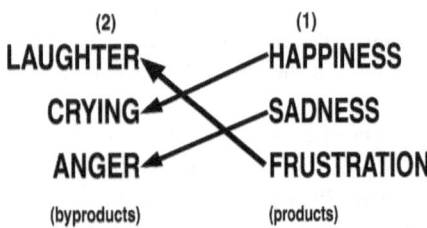

Are you into this? This is wood. Roots and all. Mix and roots. Show some credibility. We are all mixes. But the catch is this, 100%. Everyone of this and us is so close to being 100% of one of one. That a politician's heaviest breath could only move a decimal point. And that's barely enough. This seems like idle shit talk. What this proves is this. It grows in, around and on you like roots. No matter how hard you pull it won't come done clean out. Your 100% (with the occasional byproduct 2 floating to the surface for masking) is there to ring. Ring like wood's leaves in the wind. I am one thing in my in the beginning. I am 100% ANGER. With foolish sadness floating up and around. Production is my anger hate so fuck you my beginning is here. My wood is here and everything's in order in my in the beginning.

Congratulations. Honest. I am ready. Muscles tensed. Mind at ease. Fire in my mouth and ring in my eyes. Congratulations! The beginning has begun on a negative affirmation. To show truth (truth will be represented later in this life) I am tangents everywhere. My topics are spread. So be prepared, sense is only in the beginning and at the ending. So until then. Stomp the concrete, take the meat, pull the wood and remember, take it or leave. Are you ready? I am. For my project to begin. Now is the time to explain the project. Now is the time. No time. In me. The time that I build. My project I build. Are you ready? I am. I love adventures.

Build her.

-PROJECT-

Dim light corrodes my mind. Sitting in my corner with my dim light soothes me. For my teeth are rotting. Nothing shocks me. Everything shocks me. The idea of her glowed pink. Pink dots are nothing once they are worked out. Just bugs.

I wear my shoes and glasses to sleep. So when I jump out of bed to work them out. Pink bugs. Pink dots. The glasses are to protect me from the dim light. Shoes for the shock of the jump. Because. That's when I am most open is when I lay. Lay to think of soothing or rotting. Shocks of dots. Soothe and rots. Damn pink dots. Must be worked out. If not I sell myself out. For real CHEAP. That's shock number one. Shock number two is her legs. Dots and shocks, man. I need weakest and strongest, respectively. I want weak dots so I can move on (see what I mean: CHEAP). Strong shocks are for the better things to write about. She asks for it all in her legs. For she is natural. This is natural 100% no mixtures here. Except for the plaster but that's for later. A juicy morsel for you to wait on.

I've spat truth at you for some reason. Respect this. This is respect. The truth of reflection is...

I am getting ahead of myself. If I may suggest, that by writing all this down quick about her you may think. Think it took me a brief moment to build and create. It didn't and don't you forget it. The wire and the concrete alone prove that. That it meant something. So of course it took some time. Months. And don't you forget it, man. Man is, you are, nothing to her. Wire has encased her legs, started her off. Even without knees we should (who says should)all bow to her (tradition says so). Bow and beg for mercy from the should tradition. And especially MAN. Woman is one with her. But woman should still bow because she is part of the problem. But man is the bigger problem. We are a big joke.
Man is a big joke with our penises hanging out. We show off. Laugh, fight, curse and act tough. I guess they're all the same. Almost. Tough is tough. We all laugh, figh,t curse. Woman and man. But only man gets tough. But this is all nothing to her. And that's why we should all bow (especially man, and don't you forget it) and beg for mercy. It's nothing to her. A joke to her. That's why she laugh so hard.

It's self-explanatory, the title of this split of a split second says it all. It also spells quickness. She screams for me to be quick. And I'm not even half way. That's fine, though. When she screams, I pain. It hurts so much. But that's alright. Pain is what she is. Quick harsh pain.

Pain so much. I can't move around. My replacement parts are free. That is BAD. A bad let down. Waste. Think around the pain to her and what she could be and most importantly, will be. Will be.

Self self self. Herself and myself. Slow tracking with blood and dust in my eyes. What's in hers? I'm not sure. She's not really born. No parental advisory necessary here. You and everyone else know what they are getting into. The title of this epitaph says it all. This tomb my tom,. is dreadfully alone. Does this add or detract from her birth? No. No, no detracting from me. I add she detracts. Subtracting.

I told you, it's an <u>adventure!</u>

Decisions and laws of nature. Decisions are mine to make. And she is the law. Because my screen TV told me. And I believe it. I've seen it many times. Life's a bitch and then you murder one. I say murder. Because marrying is narrow. You know it's a female because I am male. I do not see males like females. They are different. I am for both. But (for me) marry is for me. And murder is for all of the above. I told you, decisions and laws. My decisions make my laws. Not the other way around. But her decisions make my laws. This is why I say murder, it's for both male and female. Ambiguity. She has fame and I am anonymous.

Why is this important (don't be sarcastic, I'll kill you?)? This is why. I could marry her (I already had near the end)but murder is more productive. I murder her every time I touch her or caress her. And she does the same to me. I could not marry a male. I would feel low and sold out to myself. But males have made their law (to female or male). And I respect this.

But murder is different. Clean effective. It takes no prisoners. See what I mean. No. Oh well. I can't hand-feed you. And you can't do the same to me. I must live with all this. And the final punch line.

I could not murder a female I have married. If I did (physically or mentally) I would end myself. That's why this is important to my adventure project.

I must rest. I have to clean. For I am tired. Her leg wires are near completion. Sleep shock comes now.

I rise. With this fact comes another reality. I want to please you. Everyone wants to please someone. Whether they admit it or not.

This is real, I am real, I admit it. You don't. So my reality (everyone's reality, really (no pun intended)) is bitter. Bitter to you, bitter to me. But I have grown accustomed to the taste. You. Have not. You. Mask it. My way and your way are both not living with it. One is habitual, one is a farce. With this tender fact, I rise. With her I rise.

I do her knees. They are almost as important as her chest, and arms. The chest and arms for later. I don't mean to tantalise you (no sarcasm please) but that's the way it must be.

Knees for her support and flexibility to my tantrums. I don't even know her and I already love her. This happens often with me. Not usually with shes (plural, there's many). I look at a woman's hair, eyes, stomach, back and knees. No porter will direct me through this. I have to do it alone. With her, it is alone. That's why I know my love is real. Even now. With many others I am a loser nothing in front of many. It's been close sometimes.

Right now, as I write this after the truth fact (yes truth, is back like a virus) it's (love?) the closest it's ever been. This is a small fact truth. So it's hardly a factor in this game (yes, a game, life, love, hate, all a silly game). But I have to state it, the fake love to the pretty woman has increased the obesity in me and in her. It has made her stronger but me weaker. Only she makes me strong. So we must murder and marry at some time.

I must slow myself. The knees are barely stable and the thighs have begun. I must relax myself. Calm. Legs. Have you noticed how strong your legs are? I mean, legs are almost twice as strong as your arms. I get this in my head. Even if you are an 80 pound weakling your legs are twice as strong as your arms, amazing!!

You use your legs so much they are, they have to be like a natural. Wood concrete, but at this stage she and me are wire. The choice of weightless champions. If I could I would walk with my arms. So they would be just as strong as legs. Then I would be even. Even is important for me. I will speak of this later.

Her legs must be as strong as her arms. For legs are for standing solid. Arms are for grip crushing. For a crushing grip. This had to be said. Now, we shall move on with us.

She watches me even unfinished. She is just a trunk. I haven't started wood yet. To recap, it's now just wire. Vultures are low and black and waiting to pick me up if I fail. When I fail. For I will. I will explain.

The three is back. Beginning, middle and ending. Birth we are one, death we are one. Life. Life is failure. Must be. Because we are many. This is not right. My mother born me so. So if in life there are many. Does this mean we just use people to pass time? I'd like to hope nay, to accept failure and to hide it is failure. So is life failure? I try to be alone but I fail and need other people around. Is this failure?

I can't find it. I am lost. I think no one can find. If so and you do, know secrets, reach for me. I won't hang you. Promise. Please reach for me. I want and am dying. Promise please? Please promise.

What's wrong in me? I can't know it. Can't I? I'm scared. Deathly frightened. Her head beginnings are complete. I put the wire around my face, enlarged it and now she is a trunk with a head.

I'm not frightened of her and how you will react if you see it. I'm frightened of what I'm writing. I'm scared I'm exposing too much of myself. To myself and to you. Will you be original as you see (read) this (me)? Or will you smile and turn your head? For the first time I am scared you'll hurt me because of who I really am. Not what's on the outside. I have brought this on by bringing out onto paper from ink. The ink is blood being drained from my finger from my head. It all goes onto paper. Which is my chest. My nail on my right index finger is long. So the blood from my finger/head mixes in with the engraving. Mixes in with the blood from my chest.

How will this work? Have you figured what I'm trying to do by writing this down?

It's a case history about what I endured creating her. And how I feel after the end. The end. It's a long way till we reach that light at the end of my tunnel. For better or for worse. Till death do us part. Part us do death? We'll see.

I'm trying to help myself. Cure my ailment. But my thoughts get mixed and messed up like a computer with a virus spreading its wave in it. Bear with me and I'll try and bear with you. I think you can help me! Isn't that NEAT! By inputting your virus into me, I think it could help me.

Save this for later. For her memory awaits me. I can't even speak the name.

I do know she will be beautiful but extremely ugly. Trustful, yet full of writhing lies. She sees through me and she sees through you. She is not holy. Her arms to embrace you are not embodied in me, on me on her. Her chest with its obscene growths. They are not breasts. That is a lovely word. She has tumours on her outside where ours are in the inside. But we love her anyway.

Sometime around here she started kicking and screamin. at me. I needed to get part of her now. Already I saw I was beginning to become a bit of a slave.

She needed dirty magazines for the woman's tits. I say "tits" because I find this is an obscene word. And for my sake the more obscene I made her, the better. The better. Better it was and will be.

I had this short friend and he said he had found a whole batch of these "smut mags". So he gave them to me to <u>dispose</u> of. After I was finished though, I threw them out. He seemed disappointed at the fact. I felt bad and thought I should go buy a bunch more and give them to him. But I changed my mind. First I couldn't get my balls up (or down depending on your perception) to go buy some more of the magazines. Second, I thought he might get offended. Like, I was implying he didn't get "laid" enough. And third I didn't think I owed him (or anybody else) that much. I mean it wasn't for me. It was for her. So what anybody thought at this stage was small and not to be considered. An alien thought was no size to eat.

I remember (memory, not feel or felt because I could not feel any of this then or now) looking through the magazines for the "tits" and needing to put it aside because my eyes hurt, throbbed. Just like my hand and guilt. I could only do this in the early morning. I was paranoid(I still am paranoid)that someone saw or had seen or had felt "that perverse little boy cutting out titty pictures from the dirty magazines".

This whole process was time consuming and horribly sickening. I was poisoning myself and didn't even realise it. This was the hardest part of making her, making out her. Making out with her.

The magazine cutting hit made me think of an incident when I was in grade 10. Grade 10 was four years ago from <u>her</u> present. Tack another two and you get <u>our</u> present. These past two years from her beginning <u>are</u> tacked on. Tacked onto my chest and arms like a tag on a cow's ear. Painful but tolerable.

In grade 10 in my "Creative Writing" class we were told to cut pictures from magazines and write down why we cut them out.

I decided to go through 50 to 100 magazines (main picks were TIME, LIFE and PEOPLE) and pull out every photo that implied sexuality and violence. From someone pointing a gun to war. From a women with a low cut dress to a picture from a scene from a skin flick.

Needless to say I ended up with a lot. I think I filled a one and a half inch binder.

My teacher did not find it amusing. My point was not taken. Amusing. I can't remember what the point of that was. My point is almost always not taken. So I guess it doesn't matter.

More pink dots. She is black. It is meant to be that way. My memory points are pink dots and so is going through these rags. Pink dots do not fit with her. She tells me so. She tells me pink dots are problems.

My memories make sadness float up and corrupt her. So I think of her tumours on the outside and ours in the inside. So I think I must lay. Even though she is headless and armless (it doesn't matter, she is still strong) I will let her rest. While I do some resting too.

At least I am done with our magazines. My eyes are very sore. I will tape them up. And nail them shut. So my dreams and body do not do anything with my hands.

It probably won't work.
It saddens me.
It rests me.
I rest.

It didn't work.

My mind and body both betrayed me. They always do. Betray. Betrayal. My mind is a trap. Quick and strong. For you and me. My body is a service for my mind. It works with it and against it. The same with my mind.

They betray me and everyone else.

She doesn't know this and never will until the end. When I trap her like I did in the in the beginning. I trapped her to create her. She doesn't know this (if she does, then she hides it well) and never will. Until the end. Because. Every set of lovers have their secrets kept from each other. Mine is a different case. She will figure it all out at the end. If she knew now her arms (mobile arms) would trap <u>me</u>. And crush <u>me</u>. So I have secrets. She has hers. If she finds out mine at the end. I will most definitely find out at the end. That scares me. Not her. It doesn't scare her.

That is her gift. Not mine.

I avoid her secrets like I avoid bad tasting food. With all my senses shut.

Not her. That is her gift. She doesn't know my secrets. She does know she will eventually find them out. She is not scared. She is casual about them. So she waits, for she knows. She knows when I hurt her. She will hurt me twice as much.

So she waits.
Relaxed.

So I wait.
Frightened of the pain.

That was then. This is NOW.
You who already scowl. You who all think you are all. You who aren't. Scorn my ideas and try to foul us. You are the lowest common denominator. What you have is others' opinions. Shallow and hollow. You are. You insist on knocking me. Knocking me down when you say you don't care. What you don't realise is, you, you fuel me. You fuel me. You drug me. You are my drug. You stick it in me and pull it out just as fast. Anger is speed. Anger speeds me. Anger is my speed. Depression is my hangover. You enjoy all the commotion. Watching me do the junkie dance.

What you don't realise. You don't realise that while you weaken me she grows stronger. To hold me up. Fuck you. You mean, meant, meaning, mean so much to me. And you tear at me. I am no commodity. You will not sell me like you sell everyone else. I will show you. I will show you her when the time is right. When the time is right I will show you, her (me), and you laugh. When you leave you will stop your fucked in, up game. And continue it a step further. By saying to your hyena friends, your jackal friends, "He is not right". You will say this to your animal friends around your roasted prize on a camp fire that I am not right. You roast all the emotions you have killed with your gossip slurs. You roast me. You kill me.
i will kill you.
I WILL KILL YOU.

SHE will kill you.
She will do this because my shroud is on. Even just a wire foundation. Not half done, she is my strength. Even though I create her (and that takes strength) there are somethings I can't bring myself to do. With or without my shroud of sad on. On me. I don't have much (any?) support now. Now, and most certainly I didn't have any (much?) support then.

I just can't seem to find my own foundation. Everyone else's, every thing else's support, yes. Me no and not only, lonely. Lonely. Not only am I lonely, I find no friend in my writing anymore.

You may think I'm getting off topic here. I'm not. I am not. Everything I do becomes a part of me. She does, work does, a writing. It's just that some things I do or say, grow from me. Grow away from me. And I am left alone. Count on me to be alone. Count on me to be scared to talk to a female about getting closer. Count on me to screw up again. Count on me to get nothing out of my life. Count on me to never relax. Count on me to be a loser. Count on me to sleep when it's time to figure out my problems.

Count on me.

Count on me to go for a rest.

Like her three sides, I too have three sides. Hers are equal but some only see one or two. You will be the judge, jury and skeptic in the future.

I have three main sides. Anger, Sadness, Content. Anger and Sadness rule over Content. Some say that's sad but I am most productive in Anger and Sadness. I am lazy when I am Content. That's why I think it's sad to be Content.

Sort of.

Being Content I remember and see my surroundings. See and remember my surroundings better than if I was in Anger or Sadness. So I don't really mind being Content.

Content I feel small freedom.

Sadness is from me not realising my freedoms. Sadness strikes then. Not really strike but slowly swallows me. Like when you eat ice cream for the first time in eons of years. You suck on it slowly and it slides down. That's how Sadness comes to me. Comes on to me.

Comes on to me and I am left open.

Left open to be ridiculed by "people" (animals?) who have no concept of what it's like to be hurt this hard. Anger comes at this point. Anger comes at this point when I try to think of my ideas of freedoms. And my ideas of freedoms are infringed on.

I take my freedoms seriously. They are my dreams. I wish to be peaceful and free in my way.

I had this friend in an old group of loser friends. She always used to have sex with a different guy each weekend. I guess she was considered a slut (I hate that word). In a way she might have found her freedom by doing that sort of thing. Now I hear (heard) she has a steady boyfriend friend boy. Now maybe that's her freedom.

We all change so much that I wonder if I (or she) notice changes in us at all. Or maybe I'm just full of shit.

Sometimes when I'm content I am happy.
Sometimes when I'm content I am not.

Changes, elaborations and mutations. They happen all the time. Changes and freedoms. Happen. I'm worried what freedoms (changes) tomorrow will bring. And how I will see them (if at all) once I'm through scraping my face on the wall.

Perceptions changes your views. Views and perceptions. How I view my percept once I've wounded myself must not be taken into account. If not my tomorrow will not exist.

Sometimes when I am happy. That is when I realise what I am doing. What I am doing to myself. What I am doing to myself could be called defeatist. Creating something that slowly eats myself away. The reality surrounds and corrodes me. It is truth. It is truth. It is truth. It cries as it devour my innards.

Is this ego?

NO.

Some people mistake truth with ego and ego with truth. No, there is no ego here. My back door is always open to the different cries of truth. You had better believe that or lies will devour <u>YOU</u>. I think it is better to be eaten alive by truth than buried alive in a snake pit by lies. When I seek truth I find pain and hunger. But with this I always find truth. All the pain and hunger I have gone through to find truth. Makes the find of truth more worthwhile. When I find truth I am content. And sometimes when I am content I am happy. That's why I do this. That's why I do her. To find truth and be content. To be content and happy. This is a refining process. By the end we shall be totally refined. The end. Refine. Refined.

Concrete. It is time for concrete. The wire is done. Concrete must be now put on. She needs more strength. She needs all the strength she can get to stand up to my expectations. She accepts the expecting of my expectations. As I do hers. Except. Excepting exempting others expecting expectations is important. They distort me and mine. Expectations.

Lovely.

Lovely. Why do I do so ugly? Why do I do so ugly. Why am I so ugly to people. I am not my penis? My penis is not me! Fuck you. I am my one. Lovely. No cult here. No one follows me. I am not a penis. That is why. That's why. I am not muscle either. I am small wire. No format to me. That is why. I am not.

Lovely.

That is why I am not lovely. I am ugly for I am to my mind what some people are to their penises and muscles. That is lovely in our world's story. So that makes me ugly. That is the truth. Truth is back. Because. Because we all lie to ourselves and call it truth. We all lie. Every second of every year we live. So we believe ourselves truths. But they are lies. Cover ups. We lie to cover up? Yes. We do because we are all insecure of something in or around ourselves. That's why we close our eyes when we kiss. So we don't see something in the other person that makes us insecure. Or uglies us. Or uglies them in our perceptions and views. We close our eyes so we don't see our reflection in the other person's eyes so we won't feel insecure about ourselves.

That is why we have sex in the dark. So we can't see others imperfections. See the other's imperfections and we will feel (we feel) small and sad and ugly and alone. That is why we masturbate in the dark. So we can't see our own imperfect actions. All of the above has been mentioned because we are all negative toward each other. Negative to see only imperfections and feel insecure about our ugly selves.

We are all ugly some way or another.

I have accepted this and I still feel insecure about mine and everyone else's imperfections. Negative. A lie. A truth. Imperfection. Insecurity.

How do you work with all these pieces mashing in on one another. Desperation.

We get desperate. And the odd one kills himself. Suicide is not an act of bravery or of cowardice. It is an act of desperation. Hopelessness. When all of the above's harsh truths (harsh lies?) crashes on you. When you have no support. Suicide is viewed as an imperfection by most others. Thus it is ignored. Thus the suicidal is ignored. Thus we are all ignored. Thus we all ignore. While someone dies.

I have thought of my suicide.

I have tried my suicide.

I have failed my suicide.

Many fail. So they go on to find a purpose. Some do. Some don't. I think I have. My lie truth in her. My lie truth I have created in her. Concrete. First stages of it is a truth (lie). Until then I must accept my expectations. Her expectations (accept only hers because mine and hers are the only truth (lie)). Excepting, exempting other's expectations. Ignore all muscles and penises. Stand with the mind. Store loveliness in the dark. Open ugliness to the light. And chain imperfections and insecurities together in a negative cage. Far from me. And most importantly. SAVE MY DESPERATION. For other times. It along with the other impurities, I have debriefed you on, for another time when my purpose is complete. Until then.

Back to my war.

Concrete. School. Rewriting.
Let me tell you how they fit together.
Like the pieces of a puzzle, they are all different.
Let me tell you how they fit together.
Rewriting.
I never do it.

I let it come on to me. Like I'm sitting on a cloudy beach. At the exact moment the sun shines down on me, a wave of water goes right over me.

That's what it's like when I write. It slides in on over me and pulls me to look at myself. Look at myself and tell me what's happening to me. Around me. In me. So I write. So I flow. So it flows. That's the best way to explain it. I just flow it. It flows me. It flows with me. I flow with it. Me flows with it. It comes out of me like sweat. I sweat when I write. It is work. But it is not work. It's more fun than work. But work can be fun. But rarely is. More of my work. More of work later. <u>MUCH</u> later.

What was I saying. What was I saying? I was saying I write what I flow. With. With me. I write what I flow with. Sweat. So why should I rewrite? Why should I rewrite. I shouldn't. Scratch that idea write (right) out. To rewrite would be to distort my vision. My visions. Why should I do that? Why should I do that. I shouldn't. Leave it the way it is. Then I know I am sincere about myself and everything I write about. Flow about. Float about. This idea keeps me afloat.

Concrete. Has to be like a town. A cool town.

It must. They must have pockets of air to keep it comfortable. To keep it afloat. But remember it is strong. Concrete. Just concrete. Not city. A city uses concrete. Thus a city becomes impure. But again, it stays cool just like pure concrete.

I am pure concrete.

I can float.

I can float because I have air pockets to keep me alive. To keep me afloat. The air pockets are my writing. I need no doctor to tell me that. Fuck you. Fuck doctors. They can write their medications but it won't help me. Concrete. Concrete doctor. That's what I am. A concrete doctor. I write my own prescriptions to make me feel better. To make me feel breathing. To make breath air. Air pockets. To breathe with. To stay floating (afloat) with. Concrete with air pockets. No towns. No rewrites. Just written concrete. I am just written in concrete. To learn from myself. Because concrete only fades when it wears out and that won't be for awhile. For until we (she) are (is) done.

Written in concrete to learn.

Learn and schooling. Schooling and learning. Learning to live with. Schooling. Learning to live with school. What you learn in school is like eating and shitting. After a teacher teaches you. You don't need it anymore. So out it comes. Eating and shitting man. I shit out and on the teachers because they taught me very little.

So there was nothing I could put out. For them. For them for me. Just for me. I am my own teacher. I have taught myself to write. I am shitting my own knowledge out. To make myself a better person. No school teacher could do this. Three years after my schooling and it's still scarring me. Scarred me.

Feeling embarrassed to write this way in school. Any school I was in I felt like asking the fat man with the school teacher who just taught shit food. What he wanted to do with all this. To make himself better. To get a job. To get work? Oh well. To each his shit teacher own.

I am not saying I didn't learn anything from the fatman and those teachers.

I did.

But it was so small it had very little influence on me. I was my own influence.

I was my own influence and I still am. My cranium is. One time written. Pure air pockets concrete. Self teacher schooled. My cranium is this. My point is this. If I was to use school teachers knowledge on impure concrete with no air pockets and rewrite it. The pages would curl onto themselves and see and mean nothing to me myself and I. I would be another type sell out. Like a lie sell out. Like the cheap sell out I mentioned before. Which is now history.
You have to understand that after every word second passes. That is now history.

That is why I need concrete. It is somewhat permanent. It only wears out when it is finished with. Understand.

Understand that's why I need concrete. When it starts chipping off. When she starts chipping off. She is completing. And becoming <u>boring.</u> This must be stopped in the first stages. I must stop now. Before I give the ending away. This is my secret. Like I said before. It is an adventure with a surprise at the end. So the rest comes on, onto me again.

She needs more concrete.
I need more rest.

Oh, if I could stay up and complete her in one swipe. But I know she wouldn't be anything like I want or she wants to rush. But I will cut it short. I am close to finish? Am I? My body wants to rush. But I will cut it short.

I noticed I only look at her in the dark. Sort of like the dark I spoke of earlier. If it seems I am getting off topic. But everything I speak of, spoke of relates. Relates to her. Relates to me. Whenever I do something that I feel is trustworthy of myself and my emotions and my feelings it is part of me. She is part of me. I am part of my emotions my emotions are a part of her. Her, me, emotions. Art (?), me, emotions. All one part. All three parts. Interchangeable. This had to be said. So it is known that I am not rambling. This will be spoken more soon. Ending near. Near ending.

Fuck you and the horse you rode. A few have seen her in the final stages of plaster (concrete). And have already judged her. They are mixed but she is 100%. So you have no right to judge her natural concrete (plaster). Go pick at your feet. Don't piss on me. Your horse doesn't make you look triumphant. Pick at your feet while you walk. Make sure you can walk. For that horse doesn't become you. You don't even have a flag to bear. To raise. To raise a point. She is unfinished.

She is unfinished. Leave her alone. Leave me alone. Your spurs just upset me. They don't pain me along like they do your horse. Do your horse. They do your horse. everyone does. Everyone says what you say while you hide your flag. Keep it hidden from anyone else. You hide it because. Just because. Because you are scared.
Because.
BECAUSE YOU ARE SCARED OF HER.

The rest is fast. Short spurts. Quick! Quick! Quick! Run let the bass kick. All right! In an angry tone. Do you know we are all organised clowns. Putting on our make-up and clothing every morning. Gotta get at that real world. Attack all those rumours. And get ahead while your drunk. Yes drunk on your paycheck. To scared to push back when the boss bullies you.

Well, I'll tell you, when someone pushes me, I push back twice as hard. Fuck you and your eyes. I can't. I can't stand it when you stare at me that way. There is no kings road. That was roughed up years ago. The concrete had to be done in news. Research. Researcher it had to be done. I am nothing. All right. Concrete must be done needfully quick in our world. Break out. If not then she would change to something else. That would be horrible. No need here. No fucking gas. No gas needed. I'm already dead. Fuck you. You're enjoying this. Right yes. A thousand miles an hour. Boys will be boys. I will name once this is something. Once this is nothing.
CONCRETE IS COMPLETE.
DONE.

He is nothing to me. Me is nothing to me. You are something to me. I cry to admit it. Because. Nil. Because. Because you don't care and neither do I that tomorrow is nothing. Tomorrow is too much. I am too much. I wish I were dead. But wait till freedom dies. Freedom comes with wood and magazines. They taste too good with pillows. They make it too soft. And magazines are too rough and bitter. You don't know. But I am crying while I write this. It is pain and me. No blast. I cry. No one really listens to wood. No beat. No care. I must crash and burn.

Cut and cut. Tear and tear. Tear to tear. I am nothing. She is nothing till my pain is evolved. You can not imagine how much pain I go through. Just to make (me) her or anything else that <u>some</u> people consider art <u>some</u> people consider me.
Me. Me. Me. Me. Me. Me. Me.

Modern nothing art looking green?

No romance in a bad situation. I am that romance and bad situation. Unfortunately I don't (is this so bad?) I can't I try to seduce people.

Wood is not romantic. It is frantic truth. Head. My head is screwing tight. I'm not sure which is present or past. White teeth and suits. Nothing fits at this point. Rewriting will be (divine?) necessary. I am scared to ask anymore. For I feel am am asking too much. I am someone else too much. I am I am myself too much.

Washing it's too fast. Pasting. Slapping. I can't tell how loud it is. I want to tear (cry). But I don't know how to anymore. No rebel. I stink with no living, no life and no drink in birthright. I need a green field and this is not doing it for me with long hair and no hair or dog or god or money or whine. I will not push it in. I already have. Her mouth is puckered and black and red and I am writhing on the floor MINE free sunset she her face are almost done with minimal damage or depression or wealth or fame or god

You will see my blood in her and I have died to do this. Repeat repeat to your side of this you are not me me is not you beat is not you or me and she is not anything of the above remember the above it will come much faster than I can write. So look listen and learn hear it comes.

I will sleep on my floor now. Thank you very much. Now. Killing. Killing myself I am a joke.

Commodities to no inspirations. Rest.

No. I don't want to act so much but all of it is coming so fast and it will be screamed in the end soon you will know why I do this.

Rewriting is no inspirations. Rest.

Rewriting is NOT Divine and NOT necessary. Rest.

Commodities to no inspirations. Rest.

Concrete complete. Wood begins and ends. This was the quickest part. Taking all the moods and putting them into her. All into her. All onto her. All over her. Organised and disorganised. The blood is there from one night. Last night. When I was not myself. But I wasn't. I was. Was. I wanted to hold her. Not the one. But another her and touch her hair. Would this have distorted the one her? I don't think so everything I do or did in this or that time is in her. On her all over her.

Basically what I am (have) doing (done) now is putting into her. Onto her. All over her is what I seek and feel around me, on me, into me and all over me. Understand? News and papers. With blood, sex and addictions in them or her. Understand.

Completing a project is the most confusing. Completing a part of myself is the most confusing. It is the most fulfiling.

I want to grasp to hold and to burn down. And up. I look at her in the dark. She shields me. What went and is going into her disgusts most civilians. Congratulations! The beginning has begun on a negative affirmation. To show truth (truth will be represented later in this life) I am tangents everywhere. Right? Yes the truth has been represented fully. Right. Like I've felt and said, I love adventures. Especially the ones that go into myself. Most of the pink dots, errors, misjudgments and wantings are gone. Remember, this is natural a 100%, no mixtures here. And you have to respect it, that. Even when you hide what you really feel by scanning this. Even then this could be more organised by people's standards. So of course my calling will be others hiding. Now I am begging you to listen even though killing myself over and over again is boring. Bear with me, My adventure is almost over. I can't rest now. I have to keep risen with this facting fasting fast reality. Remember, we all have reasons for doing things. The reasons are pretty much the same for anybody. But the results are different. But most people won't say it. Even me. I just use props and let you try and figure it out. I'm not strong enough. My legs are not too strong like Her's. But I guess it's just birth (starting of the race), life (failure) and death (the big prize for failing the race), right? Right. Race and bear with me and everyone else. Life is a failure. A denial call to the finish. But no one makes it out of this race alive. Or without scars. That's failure. Failure not to protect ourselves better. We are all failures of some sort. Death is the prize. The surprise (how I love surprises) for failing. Failing means nothing to no one but yourself. Everyone else is a zero. This is no sin. Some sin. Sin on a sin. I have not sinned for helping myself. Period. You will see. Needles in pink dots and blackness. Saddens me. Rests me. Wrests me. Into rest. I am her now. She will kill my now and your then. Chew on that conceptual plant while it grows out of its foundation into yours. Don't know what I will do? Want to? Want do. Will do. In you? Sometimes when we look at each other we are content. Sometimes when we're content we look at each other differently. Different.

Difference. No ego around. That makes a big difference in all of this. I am not my penis. That makes a different difference here. It makes all sort of dark and indifferent. That's why suicide is out of desperation. It's not noble or cowardly. It's desperate measures for desperate times. Times is now. Are now. The time is now and suicide must be put away because my work is so fun. I love this adventure. It might just make a concrete school for me to learn about myself in. That. That. That I can learn how to teach fatman and teachers about my interchangeable parts. The emotions and all. All. All. All of me? Hopefully. But I am (we all are) quick to let the bass kick up my (our) defenses. While we make it soft. It soft. Us soft. On soft inside. Our insides are made soft. Modern nothing art looking green? Looking green at frantic truth (her) will make you see (her) red black blood. I have not rewritten anything. Results are the result of concrete sleeping on the wood with the wire. Completing a her project is the most confusing. Especially when I've got her name.

---

society's grip

SARAH

S ick
A lienation
R eceived
A t
H ead

Sarah. Her name is Sarah. I have to call her this so as to get personal with her. Now that it's necessary. We are all personal with her. Her grip. Its grip. Society's grip. The grip it holds onto us. Claiming that if we play by its rules we will win. Claiming that if we get one of its addictions we will win.

SEX
DRUGS & ALCOHOL
VIOLENCE
SPORTS
RELIGION
MONEY

WHICH IS YOUR ADDICTION?
I KNOW MINE.
DO YOU KNOW YOURS?

If you think you do or don't have an addiction and you are making a different difference. You will receive its sick alienation at your head. She is ugly. It is ugly. Sarah is ugly. Society is ugly. I am ugly. You are ugly. Whether we admit it or not. Whether we admit our addiction or not. This is how we are all one. We are all ugly. Sarah, Society. You, me. Hide it if you choose. That's up to you. To me I will get to me what got to her to me. I created Sarah. I created Society. So in my own small way I will destroy my part of Society. Burn my part of Sarah. Burn my part of me. Of me. Part of my addiction. Most of my addiction. For the smallest fraction is always there. Addiction is ugly. Addiction has ugly, have ugly. We all have ugly. It's just I've chosen to burn my ugly. Burn my addiction. Burn my part in Society. Burn my part of Sarah. Burn my part of me.

BURN, BURNING, BURNED

It's funny my bed felt much smaller. When I looked at it to go to sleep. Sleep came hard. Restless. Turn, Turning, Turned. I felt like crying. I felt I felt like being held onto. Without my shirt. I felt like nothing. I still feel like nothing. No one around me. To comfort me. I am sad. I am nothing. I can't sleep after I did this. I beat her. I hurt her. Her. Sarah. I hurt Sarah. I smell of death. Everything around her skeleton corpse ashes smells like that has turned over. Rotted.

Turn. Turning. Turned. I want to cry because it's almost time for me to die. My society to die. Then I will be more of a nothing. But more of a complete. A cough for me please, I am nothing. I am hungry. Hungry for me to die. It's almost time for me to die. Sarah has. Sarah died for my sins. Now I must die for her sins. I will tell you now, I'm not sure how this will come about. I think I must live to die for her sins (for my sins). Live with her sins. Live with my sins. I want to sleep soon.

TURN, TURNING, TURNED.

No sleep here. I feel like crying and then dying. I am feeling like a real nothing when a little tiny kid busts in.

"You're a baby, a big scrawny baby who wants to cry over yourself and find somebody else to help comfort yourself besides yourself. You're a NOTHING!"

Funny thing is, my mouth was (is) so dry while I did her. It's sort of sex you know. You feel relieved after your finished.

Funny thing is, there will always be a part (apart) that nags at me like this is unfinished. Funny. Not funny. Funny small dry unfinished feeling. Feeling. Nothing feeling. Funny that she was hot. The heat scorched me. But that has nothing to do with nothing. With feeling. Funny small dry unfinished feeling. Feeling. Nothing. Feeling.

-PROLOGUE-

This is not dough. Just lumped together and thrown down on wood. This takes all the strengths, of concrete and makes fortifications and foundations. That I have grasped. Three. Everything is in threes. Wood, wire and concrete. Begin, middle and end. One, two and three.

I needed something to take me from nowhere to somewhere. Nothing to something, even if it's a brief moment. A split of a split second. I want to grasp to hold and to burn down. And up. In order for my grammar to be understood all who scan (nobody reads paper anymore it's mean to be scorned and then burned) you must fall. Fall down and up and back down. Slammed hard. Proof reading is not necessary. Rereading is not necessary. Take it or leave. Leave it. And leave me running down. It means to me about the same as I was in the beginning.

Wire the three in and all together to me. Congratulations. Honest. I am ready. Muscles tensed. Mind at ease. Fire in my mouth and ring my eyes. Congratulations. The beginning has begun on a negative affirmation. Affirm. Affirmative. The truth has been told. I am guilty of everything. But I feel guilty of nothing. I will state this later. Soon later. Even if I am guilty I feel like I am innocent. But I am not. When she is in the field I have grasped her clowns. I was humoured. Humourous. Humoured. As she died on and around me. I reek of her.

What I feel is hard to express. But I shall try.

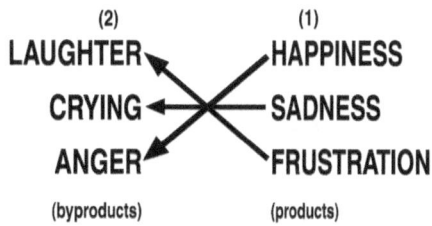

Do you understand? I guess it doesn't matter. I don't. I love adventures. I used to. I used her. I used myself. I use everyone else. I must be guilty. Even if I don't feel that way I must be nothing. Even if I do feel that way. I must remember. Even if I feel that. I must remember. Remember everything. Remember. Remember. Three, remember? Adventures of guilt in a nothing remembrance. Remember? Remember, a lot of things will go unanswered. This will not be stated again. Remember? Remember.

Remember I told you in the beginning and in the ending. Both are exactly alike. Interchangeable. Except by most people's standards the in the beginning is more organised. More acceptable. Take for instance the world. The world's end. And beginning. Beginning is a mystery we weren't around. Same with the ending. Why did it end? It's a mystery. It could very well have gone on forever, but it didn't. The beginning don't need to explain it was organised. The world's organisation in the end is profound. It's chaos. The hardest to accept form of organisation.

From hence forward. What I do is was related to her me. So whatever I do must be accepted because It's what I feel. It is a cliche. Cliche to say. I am insane. I must die.

And want to be both.
I want to be both insane and die.
And I will. I am. I was.

If telling the truth or stating facts is a sin, I am guilty (again I don't think or feel I am guilty). People have to understand that you have to live with your sins. Even though I am ill at ease with myself I have to understand this as well. <u>WE ALL</u> must understand that <u>we all</u> have to live with our sins. So live with your sins.

I do.

started this piece on
february 22nd, 1992
finished this piece on
march 29th, 1992
in edmonton, ab

#528

OUT ON A LIMB

-1-

The cry of a newborn baby reverberates off the walls and the five foot high ceiling of a hospital. The faint cries of disbelief and shock of the hospital attendants sound like muted echoes of the baby's own shrieking. One of the attendants asks, "What is it?" The little baby continues to cry and move its tiny arm and legs and head around. It is almost as if the beautiful baby boy is trying to shake off the new world he was just born into. All that the child accomplishes by doing this is to squirm and wriggle about. He is smearing blood all over the people who now hold his life. The doctor replies to the attendant's query, "I'm not sure." He elaborates, "I mean, it is most definitely a child, but I've never seen the likes of him before." The child continues to cry until he is laid down in his mother's strong arms. The mother is shocked too. She had never expected her child to look like this. She had expected a normal child like the other children. Now she doubts that her motherly instincts can help her with this child.

-2-

The young boy had just celebrated his sixth birthday last week, alone. He had very few friends at school, or anywhere else for that matter. He felt very sad. His parents had tried their best to make him feel special but nothing worked. He thanked them but he always felt a tension between himself and his parents. He always blamed himself for being twice as tall as everyone he met. He knew it was no one's fault, but this fact still did not make him feel at ease, or break the tension he always felt.

On his way to school the boy took less travelled routes so as to attract less attention to himself. He heard the muted shouts and laughter of the children playing in the school yard. Soon the boy would be in their sights and it would start all over again. It would be the same as yesterday and the same as the day before that. It would even be the same as the first day he came in contact with the other children.

He is thinking so deeply that he fails to notice two children his age come up beside him. One of the children screams out, "Stilts, how're you doing stilts!" The boy turns quickly around and down to see two other children grinning sadistically up at him. The other boy says, "How's your weather up there today stilts?" He replies, "Fine." One of the two bullies bumps into him on purpose and says, "Watch where I'm moving stilts!" They go humping along, joining the hobbling mass of small children all writhing into school.

    He waits briefly and enters after everyone else. He has to crouch to get in through the doors and move along in the hallways and into his classroom. He sees the other children half his size leaning against their desks and staring at him. He walks, ducking all of the way, to the desk that is his and sits down as low as he can get. The boy notices, just like every other day before, that everyone is staring at him. That feeling of him being late hits him again. No matter how early he comes, it's always the same. Looking around and seeing that everyone, even the teacher, is still looking up to him, he feels late. Like no one else is even in the room until he looks down. He always feels late. The student next to him pokes him in the ribs and says, "Now you're as tall as me", and starts giggling. The boy always feels late.

-3-

    The boy is sixteen years old and for the first time in his life he is happy. He just went on his first date with one of the most beautiful girls in his class, and he is in love. At least he thinks he is. All he knows is he doesn't want this feeling, whatever it is, to stop.

    He was so shocked when she asked him out, because he always thought that he was so different nobody would want to get near him. Unless they wanted to hurt him by making fun of his size. His size didn't bother her though. They went to a movie and then for dinner afterwards. It was so fun, and at the end of the evening he walked her home. They talked all the way home from the restaurant to her house and said their goodbyes and goodnights. She even hugged and kissed him! It was such a surprise that when she said to him that he should call her soon he couldn't remember if he answered her or not. She waved to him from the window in her living room, so he must have said something that was acceptable.

    As usual he chose the less travelled route home. Suddenly his happiness turns to tension and his tension turns to fear when he sees four boys in the same grade as him up ahead. He recognises them by the tone in their voices. They are some of the ones who enjoyed to terrorise him. He isn't sure what he should do. There are four of them and one of him. He slows down his pace a little, thinking that maybe he had better just turn around. On the other hand, he just can't keep on letting everyone push him around. He decides that he will continue on this path for better or for worse. That beautiful girl he had just went out with proved that not everyone wanted to push him around or hurt him. She also proved that there were some good people around. He thinks, just a little confidence is all he needs. The people like the ones in front of him are jealous, or scared, or whatever, of something that he has that they don't. He decides that if they want to start anything, he will stand his ground and then get home as quickly as possible.

One of them speaks, "Hey stilts, how's tricks?" Something inside tells him to be careful, "Fine", he replies. Looking at their arms he knows that they are into weights or boxing or something, because not many people got that strong just from walking all their life. "You know, I never would have thought that you would have come down from up there and date someone our size." The boy is very scared, "Oh." He had seen what was happening now in so many movies and television shows, but never thought it would ever happen to him. Also, those movies never even told you what to do if in real life you're surrounded and you're scared silly. "Look, I don't want any trouble. I just want to go home."

"You fucking freak, you think you're so god-damned better than everyone else." Just as the boy is going to say, "No I don't", the one who had done all of the talking, lunges for him. Without thinking the boy hits him in the groin, but not with his arms! The one who had lunged for him was down and he sees two others rushing at him. In his mind it was like a little flash of light had turned on. He now knew what they were for, and because nobody else had them, nobody else could know. A little nagging voice in the back of his head was saying, "Where's the fourth boy? Where's the fourth boy? Where's the fourth boy?" This voice though, was being drowned out by the voice that was screaming, "Get out of here!"

As fast as the two attackers are, he is faster and he easily avoids them by jumping over the top of their heads. He can't believe how fast he is moving; he had left them in the dust! Just when he thinks he is safe he remembers the little nagging voice in the back of his head. Before he can react, the fourth boy strikes him with a lead pipe across his means of escape. The heavy pipe shatters what bones are in his new found friends. He falls face first into the pavement breaking his nose and sending sparks of electricity shooting through his brain. He tastes a mixture of his own blood and sweat as he tries to hold onto consciousness. He feels his body being rolled over by four pairs of hands and in his head he is saying, "I'm late, I'm too late, I'm late again."

He hears a few clicks and the boy who he had kicked in the groin says, "We're going to cut you down to size, boy." He then realises the four assailants have knives and are all stabbing him, almost as if they are trying to carve off two of his four limbs. The two limbs that only he had. The two limbs that no one else in the whole world had, except for him. He starts to cry and move his arms and legs around, trying desperately to shake his attackers off of him. All that the boy accomplishes by doing this is to squirm and wriggle about. He is smearing blood all over the people who now hold his life. The boy who had done all of the talking and most of the stabbing says, "Now we've cut you down to our size, boy." All four boys stop their attack and leave him alone in a pool of his own blood and jumbled thoughts.

The boy feels very tired and isn't sure if he will live or die, but as he drifts off to sleep, he thinks to himself. He thinks about the movies and how they never said anything like this could happen to him. He thinks of all the trouble that his two extra limbs have caused him. And he thinks of the few good people around him, and how hard they tried to make him feel comfortable with himself and others around him. He is smiling now. He is smiling because he realises that there was never, ever a problem with him or even the good people he loved around him. The problem was with the people who caused him trouble. After going over all of this through his head, he starts to relax even more. The boy thinks to himself, "I'm not late anymore, I'm not late. They couldn't cut me down, I'm still standing tall", as he goes off to sleep.

started this piece on
april 6th, 1993
finished this piece on
april 9th, 1993
in edmonton, ab

#553

HOUR WAS

My footprints
Have been washed away
For years
My footprints
Got washed away
Years ago
To cover my past
Of years ago
I will never be able
To make that impression
Again
Our rivers
Are not for sale
A community
Planned for industry
Contradictions
All these
Contradictions
Hello
Am I welcome here?
Would you
Welcome me
If I walked up
On your doorstep
At some
Ungodly hour?
If I knew
What an ungodly
Hour was
Would you?

#400

STALEMATE

Don't like it
Ring ring
Don't be it
Die in out
Hold me
Won't touch me
Told me
Won't miss me
Then how
I care
Matters not
Matters nothing
Nothing matters
Not that
Nothing matters
Not that
Anything matters
Be me
Won't miss me
Fear
Do it
Don't do it
Do it
Just justly
Standing and
Sitting and
Holding and
And nothing
Stalemate
Standing not
Looking
Sitting not
Being
Holding not
Touching
Stalemate
Nothing
Stalemate

DO YOU KNOW WHAT DO I KNOW

I'm not sure of
What's in my head
I want to escape
Through that window
And save all of
The prostitutes
Who want to be saved
How much farther
Can I progress
Thinking like this
I need something familiar
Because everything that
I say, you
Take wrong and
It's consumed me
We have all
Seen better days
So go take a
Cold shower and
Lose the valour
And the pout
I'm not in the
Mood for it
You're not getting
Anywhere near me
Reading me my rights
You can hurt me
But you can't
Kill me
I won't let you have
That pleasure
Because that pleasure
Is saved only for me
And no one else
Don't hide behind him
He can't save you
From my word
From my word
I'd give you

My word
If you'd take it
I've been talking to
Too many strangers
You've been talking to
Too many strangers
Is the only thing
We have in common
Don't tempt fate by
Making me into the
Little boy who
Represents the new year
Don't tempt fate by
Looking at me
With that memory
When I say that
There are no more
New days
I mean it
A little more than
Everyone else
When I say that
I mean it
Decamp
I mean it
Decamp

Is that really your voice
Or is someone
Throwing their's at you
Or is it both
My body can't
Make up my mind
Because the first time
I see someone
It starts to fade away
After I see them
Several times
Do you know what I mean
All those friends
Who pushed me
Into vices and

Burned me when I stopped
I wore out
My welcome with them
And they all
Wore out
Their welcome with me
I burned
Them
I burned
Them
Just like all of those
Old friends I burned
Just like all of those
Old friends I burned
Who scorched me
Who burned me
Who burned them
Before and after I did
When they wore out
Their welcome
Old friends I burned
Who burned me
Old friends I burned
When they wore out
Their welcome
You always know

You always know
Now that there
Are no more new days
Because I'm
Damned if I don't
And even more if I do
Old friends I burned
Who burned me
You always know
That I want to
Save all of the prostitutes
Who want to be saved
You always know
I'm not sure
When most people

Believe that they
Are not worth saving
You always know
I've always felt that
Being a martyr is
Over-rated
You always know
Personally
You always know
I don't want to die
For any cause
I believe in
You always know
That I'd really wish
I could save
All of the prostitutes
Who want to be saved
But you always know
I'm too small to even
Save myself
You always know
That if I don't believe
In myself
How could I ever
Believe in anything else
You always know
You always know

#551
UNDECORATED

As the indifferent
Child of the earth
Not being the
Embodiment of
Something perfect
Not being
Subdued either
We shall sift him
Prostitute
Being male or female
We shall sift him
He is just
A figure in rhetoric
We shall sift him
Not being valenced
We shall sift him
I shall wake up
Somebody with paint
For that somebody
Will be unsubdued
As well
As all of the
Overwhelming rhetoric
Swallows all of
The indifferent
Children of the earth
We shall sift him
We shall sift

#554

THE ANT

When and
Where did it
All go
You answered
A question with
A question again
What does it all matter
Win or lose
It's all just the same
Just more rain
I want to win
Just one fight
You asked me
Why I want to
Hurt myself
I don't feel
I have to talk to you
You were telling
Me confusing stories
And I don't know why
It doesn't matter
You never wanted
To find the words
To explain to me
It was too hard
And I was too simple
When and where
And why did
It all start
In the first place
I'm never going
Home again
Why bother
It's just another
Reminder
I'm going out into
The rain
Whether it's good
For me or not

I'm all wet anyways
So I'll be camouflaged
Nobody can dance
In between the raindrops
Unless you're really small
And even then
Watch out
Because if you
Ever get hit

#493
CURTAINS

Call me by my name
Not my title
Don't call me boy
Don't call me man
Call me by my name
When you call me
Your title
You can feel my emotions
Twitch and flow and ebb
Like opening your hand
And moving it around
In a tank of oil
No one is watching
What if no one is watching
Call me by my name
Big fucking deal
No one is watching
Until that skunk
Crosses their path
Then it's the statue routine
Your title
Your title sickens me
Makes me sick
No one makes their
Own rules
You
Own rules
I'll just close
My curtains
So I don't look poetic
I'd like to think
I don't own rules
But I do we all
Own our own rules
Rules and titles and deeds
And claims
Like everyone is
Supposed to understand
Everyone else's rules and titles

And deeds and claims
And when they don't
Understand we strike out at their
Rules and titles and deeds
And claims
(There sure are a lot
 of hits going on)
And I have made mine
And sometimes
I wish I didn't
And don't and won't
But I will
I will just close
My curtains
So I don't look poetic

#569
HEAVY WEIGHT

What are you
Going to do about it?
Fill the spaces
Between my teeth
Where I bit
The bridge of your nose
I couldn't concentrate
On reading because
I was thinking about
All this so much
So much so
I had to go out
And hit some balls
I hit for so long
And hard that
My hands went all red
And they swelled up too
If only I could
Speak at you with such
Vigour and enthusiasm
One of the balls
Landed beside some thistles
And when I bent to get it
My hand got a handful
Of thistles too
I never felt the pain
If only when you
Speak at me
Your words would have
The same affect
As the thistles do
On this hot sticky day
What are you
Going to do about it
I hit a home run
While I was out there
While I was out there
I realised what a
Waste thinking about

You and your talk
And my reaction to your talk
That I went back inside
And read until
The sun went down
And I fell asleep

#525
NO TITLE

You'll never apologise
To me
It's like
Me reading without
My glasses on
I guess that's why
I don't know where
Your place is
Yes, you can say no
If yes or no
Are one of the two
Correct responses
I can't talk to you
I never could
If you never listened
It's like whatever
I said or say
Is put in a jar
To be pulled out
And spent only in
Times of need
Or for a rainy day
You said that you
Needed to take control
And I said that
My time of need
And my rainy day
Came a long time ago
What I said went unheard
Just like your apologies
That I thought were never said
Correct responses went
Right out the window
Of these haunted places
Into places that are
Even more haunted
Haunted with my revelation
That everyone is selfish
I've been reading

Without my glasses
There really was never
Going to be a happy
Ending to this story
Yes
No
The answer doesn't
Really matter now
I don't think it
Ever did
Because in addition
To me not knowing
Where your place is
You never knew
Where your place
Was either

BONDED

You
Get the fuck out of here
Get the fuck out of here
That's not an opinion
That's a scar
With a long reach
From your chest
To the across on my arms
Yes
You burned yourself
And now you scratch me
Trivialize my emotions
Will you will you not
Will you not beat me
Beat me with your opinion
Beat me till I'm angry
Me
Oh well, I'm just another
Mouth to feed or clamp shut
By myself or yourself
I'm too scared to defend myself
I don't know what you're scared of
If at all
If at all
Will
Will you will you not
Will you not beat me
Beat me with your opinion
Beat me till I'm angry
Beat me till I cry in pain and sorrow
Beat me till death
Till death do us part
Till
Till not will you not
Will you not beat me

WHAT IS YOUR FIRST RESPONSE

I could barely breath
You were stuck on me
I could barely breath
I felt some sort of pressure
To put my hand
Down your pants
Without much surprise to me
With much relief to me
My obligation that
Had been inbred into me
By you and some
Of your others
And by some of my others
Was denied
With much relief to me
You sensed my relief
And later you asked me
Why I didn't want to
If I didn't like it
My half-witted response
Was to let you into my pants
My half-witted response
Was responding to your and mine
Archetypical performance
Yes, I let you into my pants
And now that you are in my pants
Feel my hate

#445

I Feel Content Knowing It's My Last Time Dealing With These Assholes Sort Of Have No Money They Owe Me Alot Don't Matter Doesn't Eat Shit Fuck Face Don't Need Your Grief Anymore Good Luck Good Riddance Good Day For Car Meat Grass Hungry Shirt Boil Chest Boil Chest Boil On Chest Scared When She Returns To Take My Shirt Off Not Me Never Me I Feel Nothing Tape Trees Lie Down Lay Down Don't Touch My Chest I Want To Die Nothing Inside My Head Why Won't It Rain No Good Wish I Were Me Don't Know How Bus Wedding Fuck Shirt Shirts In A Bag Of Tapes Of Dreams Of Sorrow.

THE VISIT

You don't know what you're doing
Just a little boy
Murdering his father
And watching his mother burn
There's nowhere you can run
When something like this
Goes down
I want to go home
I want to go to home
I want to go to a home
It wasn't worth it
It just wasn't worth it
Where are you now?
Where are you now?
Where is everybody now
You have no right to see me
I don't have a right to see anybody
I wish I was in a band
I don't like the way you
Look at me
Look at me
LOOK AT ME!
Look at me
Look
Sooner or later
There will be another
And he'll ask you
If you remember
And I'll never be sure
Of what your answer will be

#418

PIECES

I'm going to kill the sunset
And you'll never be able to tell
Till your eyes crack
One word of hollowness
Is all it would take
I'd like to juxtapose you all
With rotten corpses
Or some small change
With pride or ego
Or both vices
You've all galvanised
My insides solid
So I'll turn you into
Some dusty piece of history
I feel like I am a
Disappointment to sports
In your eyes
But sports are all small
In mine
But I still feel your
Spurs in my sides
But the early bird
Catches the burn
I have mine
Now you'll have yours

#548
MORE OFTEN THAN NOT

While I was
On the night watch
I escaped
Down an escalator
Hard to believe
With all of the
Bad luck I've created
For myself
I got away with that

When we start touching
And getting close
And getting soft
She sometimes speaks
In my language
And more often than not
She speaks in one
That I don't understand
Life is all angles

Life is all angles
And I'm not sure of
This one
Life is all angles
This one
Special different angle
I'm not sure of
This one

Looking at the
Rich watching a boxing match
Looking at a dead tree
That was just floating
Down a river
That is now caught
In the middle of the
Same river and is now
And forever, just a perch for birds

I was never
That bastard's daughter
And I also was never
That whore's son
That was your dogma
Not mine
Life is all angles
But not your's
And not mine

VICE GRIP

Thump thump
No grip
No gripe
No rhythm
In your shoes
Or in your gaze
Pretty petty yourself
But not on me
I won't take
My shirt off
For you
I'd rather
Sweat to death
On one final
Parting grip
Of a note

Fuck you

#430

FALLEN IMAGERY

Count your penny weight
Mark your mending
Burning your imagine
Imagine
Imagining
You're with someone
In the dark
Trying to grasp
The silence
But you miss slightly
All the time
It's the best you can do
And
Marking your mend

#434

FALL IN LOVE

Desperate times
Call for a
Desperate measure
Measure your will
Will
Will you please
Step off of me
I've fallen and
I don't know
How to get up
An expanded
Formula
Why stay when
There's apathy
Yes
Yeah
Fallen in love
Fall in love
Fallen in a hole?

#435
EYES OF THE BEHELD

Moving abroad everything
She must be sold
Moving everything abroad
I must be sold
Moving abroad
We were sold
The heat is unbearable
The heat was unbearable
Beauty was heat
Beauty is heat
I've decided that
We are unbearable
Together we are
Unbearably beautiful
We are sold
But that means nothing
For beauty is in the
Eye of the beholder
And we are both blind

BUY YESTERDAY

Buyer
Stuck out in my spite
I love my
Self
Seldom
Seldom do I obey
My eyes
Or heart
Bring up my humour
Buyer
No
I shook that out
At speed
I wish I could remember
Why
Remember
Remember what I thought
Of yesterday
Of
Yesterday
But the buyer
Took me
As of
Yesterday
Of
Yesterday

#440

Thursday June 25th, 1992. I'm sitting in a courtyard outside the Winnipeg Council Building. It is overcast but the sun comes out occasionally. I'm sitting on a park bench by a large tree. No one seems to notice me. Am I invisible? I sure feel like it. I am very lonely and I want to go home to relax and think. Think about what I had. Nothing. Think about what I have. Nothing. There is someone playing an electric guitar by the dormant fountain across from me. It is soothing. I am alone now and I have nothing. I will be alone once I reach home in a little less than three days. And I have nothing. But for some reason I feel going home will be soothing. I need to be soothed. If not, I will die. And it is (or seems to be) much too soon for anything like that.

TURNTABLE TURN

I got to a shop
And had some tea
A muffin
And read
A long walk, to clear my head
(and wallet)
And I feel somewhat content
Relaxed
It's kind of strange
That minutes ago
I was depressed
And thinking of an end
Just goes to show you
How fast things can go
From bad
To worse
To good
And back all again
Like the turntable
I guess we can't
Be happy all the time
Right?

OH WELL

I just can't stand people who walk around and analyse everything
They scratch and tug and pull and tear
Being cold and machine like saying their philosophies
They say that everything I know is wrong and I am low
Their philosophies and thoughts don't mean shit to me
Being cold is not my choice, it was forced on me by these people
These people who say they are your friends but when you die it's just another specimen
They are cheap, for they will say they are hurt but in time it's just another object
One that they will scratch and tug and pull and tear
The contradiction is so big it clogs my senses
I feel like strangling
I feel like killing
I feel like nothing
I feel this way because if I die I will be a nothing specimen
I will be something just to analyse and then be discarded
A husk discarded
No longer needed, because the analogies and philosophies and bullshit have been passed
And I have failed
I have failed because I am alive
Because I am strong
And I know why they are all wrong and I have lived to tell
It's because I am cold, hard and strong (again, not by choice)
It's because everyone feels something
Everyone hears something even when there's nothing
And that's what hurts the most
These people who claim to be friends and feel nothing when you do
There's no way to relate so you die
But they will live through it because they are cold and hard
Just like me
Only they are by choice and I am not
Because I don't want to be like them
But I guess it doesn't matter anyways, we're all analysed by someone sometime
And we all analyse someone sometime

#460

SIMPLE

Crippled man
Girl with tacky earrings
Pretty female with nice dark skin
Rich man cleaning his house boat
East Indian woman sits on crippled man's hand
He looks awkward
She doesn't
Tired man gets on
Crippled man and East Indian woman talk
She looks awkward
He doesn't
Elderly man slowly leaves with his grocery bag
Art fags everywhere scowling
Alternative fags everywhere scowling
A bicycle helmet with a person on a bicycle on
An ugly green 3 ton semi
A fat lady with a slush
The mom's kid starts to cry
It all doesn't matter now
Because I'm going home

#224
SAME STRAIN

Being back in a hole
Like a "D" with no straight
Everything that's sad

Unmoving hope
Nonexistent so how
Can it move?

Taxation
Breaking point reached
Twitching and bored

It's a hard day
It's a hole
It's a hard day in a hole
It's a hole in a hard day
Flowers found discontent

Crushed and melting
Desperation and dark
Same position of numbers

I'm screaming
But I can't hear it
Someone else can!

The timely death
Is put forward again
Upside down on my hand

It's a hard day
It's a hole
It's a hard day in a hole
It's a hole in a hard day
Flowers found discontent

Death frustration suicide mercury rapid happiness pause inside joy flee die light eye time less pencil record fly no calls society crack leather cloud negate sex books nature keyboard money noise speak alcohol plastic plug liquid burst stick drugs teeth stress sexy unknown yes snake weak innocence possession remix paint love extra useless speed ditch fire food alive maybe parts river relation sketch claws help me none please feet brush suspicion young where blossom straw machine play house fight violence guilt brother caution

#492

Loyalty Is A Vice Don't Put Your Skin On Me Rest In Peace Rest Peace Rest Piece Rest The Pieces I Like The Idea Of Someone Being Scared Of Me Just As Much As Some One Looking Up To Me Low Low I Still Write I Still Wrong I Am So Wrong Obviously Obviously I Am I Am Not I Am Nothing Like You I Left A Noticed Son I Am Just Like You Rest In Piece I Should Have Cut That Off A Long Time Ago Low I Run This Is Too Long The Fat Lady Won't Ever Sing The Fat Lady Won't Sing She Forgot Her Lines She Forgot Her Lines.

#261

TECHNOLOGY SMOKE

Nature naturally Corrodes to silent fibres
Faking taut control (doesn't exist)
Plural invasions of supremacy cards
Nail and growth of flower (dirty)
Chalk lines on green define reality's fate
Numbers, formulas and plans (soon ashes)
Hole in spines are deftly disguised out
Circuits is flesh (what is flesh really?)
Soul doesn't exist anymore, so do we really?

#366

PAPER CUPS

I smell primate
I am not numb anymore
On my own side
With no limbs
I have no limbs
I gave
But I still want to
Give
Don't miss this
It will fill your cup
To the rim
I still want to give
But your connotations
Say you're too weak
To take my give
I smell primate again
I smell myself
I am numb again
With no limbs

TONIGHT WE DINE

Transmissions
Dog fights
Dog fights
Transmissions
Open and close
The heart
Dive dive
It's getting late
For those dives
Okay now picture this
Okay now I start
Chewing on your scalp
Okay now I start
Chewing on your scalp
Okay now I start
Chewing on your scalp
Munch munch
Chew chew
I'm done with
All of this
For tonight
Dog

#531

NOW

I want to go to a war
And never come back
Time may heal
But it will never explain
All of the past goings on
I started to do a painting
Just a little while ago
And it ended up that
I couldn't tell the blood
From my arm
And the paint
From my arm
From my painting
Apart
Everything's apart now
What do I do now
What can I do now
What can I be now
Now
What will happen to me
Now
What will happen to me
Now
That I can't play the umpire
Now
I can't be the referee
Now
I want to go to a war
And never come back
I'm at the bottom now
Now
I'm at the bottom
And generally speaking there's
A peace after a fight
Generally speaking there's
A peace after a fight
I want to go to a war
And never come back
I'd write to my brother

From where I am
But I don't have one
And even if I did
I don't think he would
Understand these letters
And even if I did
I don't think he would
Understand my letters
I had the peace before
Now
It's gone out
Like the blood from my arm
Or the letters from my strength
Turning my strengths
Into my weaknesses and
When I realise that
This was like some sort of a prediction
That I no longer wish
To haunt peace
But to end in a war
Now
It's no wonder why
I don't think any brother of mine
Would understand my letters
These letters
Now

#516

ROLL

And I can't even remember
Taking my shirt off
My head is being filled with lead
And my feet are now so hollow
They are both no longer
Strong, they just exist
I am no Robin Hood
The bitch is waking and
I'm keeping it all to myself
A show of glands
I've never had to worry
About a time change really
I'm not sure who she is
Because all I had to do
And did is drop the course
And I keep looking on at
Something to make sure I like it
I poke and prod at it
Like an open wound that
Itches and burns with
Its own separate mind
And I wonder if I
Keep on looking at it
If it'll change or I won't like it
I couldn't even find it
That god-damned shirt
Wasn't enough for me
You're not enough for me

THE TREE

One lone lighted tree
Standing in muddied snow
No records of park life

Stones and clouds of grey
Weeping dark patches
Of sunken, sullen snow
Broken and sad alone
No two are alike

So uncaring drab
Marble and stone
Marble and stone
Rotted wood wishes death
The real alone of waste

Alone with itself
Existence is nothing really
Alone in darkness
Death is nothing really

Pins and needles
Needles and pins
Death maybe a blessing
But no stone at all
So what's the use

#225.8
BURNING FACES

Burning faces all so crept into
Hot and scorching icicle drips
The masks are melting on children
Sabres and nickels have no meaning
No pain is no meaning of imagination
Academy of cameras are all alike
Cautious but identically strained
Perfect attire and intelligent muscles
Distribution of manufactured recordings
Thinking is a passing style for cables
Cables of trains following in sheep
You're just manufactured cases

#246

It's all negative zero to my hand
Care not for your barbed wires
Carefully noise, loud, light and static
Far from safe blankets and posters
Unsure of chairs, tables and hair
Flight patterns criss and cross
Beneath the poet and the horse
Lies light bars and glasses chain

#447

I thought I've had
To suffer
Just like any other
But I don't really
Know the time
Don't place your image
Of me onto me
I don't want it at all
I feel like cutting
My skin on my arms
Open to release
All my guilt
And loneliness
I'm tired of stumbling
Along like some
Tired old drunk
Of no use
No life to live
And no reason to look up
Just sniffling
Into nowhere
I don't like burning
Other people with
My knife
But yet if I turn
This knife around
I don't want to
Be alone anymore
I will die
I hope soon
But I'm not
So sure anymore
Sure of anything
Definite anymore
I thought I've had
To suffer
Just like any other
That's a pretty
Definite statement
Situation

When you don't know
Or even care
What time it is
An image created
By someone else
Is very definite
Is very unlike me
But trying to look up
When someone wrong
Is looking down
Is a hard task
And my head is
Too tired to bother
To look up from
The mess of nothing
I have created

FORGET TO FORGIVE

I don't want to write
When I'm thinking
I am small
Everyone thinks they're
Brilliant in some way
I'll just take off my shirt
And figure it out
I am not down
I am not down
I am not down
I am brilliant in some way
I am not
I want a picture
Of this so I can look at it
When I am not so cold
And I'm up
Slowly slowly slowly
Slowly
Imagine solid water
Someone I know well says
Notice it has a form
And if you swam in it
And you got too close to an edge
You'd fall right out
I need a request
I need my request
Forgive me
I need a request
I think I'm dying
Forgive me
I am not a crook
Forgive me
I am not a Nixon
I am not myself
I am not
Forgive me not
Forget me
Forget me a lot
Forgive me and

Forget me
Forgive me and
Forget me not
Forgive me and
Forget me a lot
Where's my shirt
And that damn photo

#403

HOOKED

I don't want to bother
Talking about you and me
I find it so hard
To see through my barbed wire
And I'm never in
My proper place anyways

My chest is not bare
And never will be to you
Money and flesh
Are not enough for me
A southern lizard
Is what you are

Missing your underwear
And your conscience
My letter of resignation
Is not enough for you
You want my blood
For payment of services

I don't value your
Services or your bond
I am not a
Buy sell trade item

#507
MASTURBATING

I got played for a disease
I got played like a disease
I feel like shoving wax into my ears
Because people who talk
Don't get asked to do encores
You have to have an instrument
And I've always been missing that
Or if I had one it always seemed
Like my hands should be laid
Totally bare and open and raw
I just want to get even
My hands are so raw
No one thinks that's even
I never get the job
Or the wax or the encores
Just a disease
Just the disease
Just myself
And I play with myself

#542
TO SEE

My quest to be
Better than average
At something
Pulls the hairs
Out of the back of my neck
Scratching it all up
Till it's raw
My tides can turn
On a dime
I can and have
Started eating the eggs
That I said
I would never eat
It's like I have
Just seen a side of you
I was never supposed
To see
Let go of the
Sad one first
Always let go of the
Sad one first
I will never need
That tree
I will never need
That tree anyways
Everything will rot and dive
Anything important
No, it wasn't anything
Good luck
And good bye
You can't lead
Me through oblivion
You can't lead me anywhere
Only I can
And it's all still
Coming at me
Grinning all the way
Like it knows
I know

That I won't
Be able to handle it
When it hits me
I see

#356
TICKET TO WEAKNESS

A little touch-up of paint
Won't matter
It's not what you apply
It's how you apply it
The punishment fits the crime
Of the abuse
Of the abusers and ignorers
Your lips are so red
Eyes so brown
But your talk is cheap
Cheaper than dust
And my paint won't help
Me make you more accessible
Because it's not what you apply
It's how you apply it
My, it's my talk
And my application is weak
Because the abuse scolds me
And my mixed sense says
You are the abuser
And I should be at
The very least the ignorer
But I'm not strong enough
To administer the punishment

DIFFERENCE

I want to be able
To recognise the
Dancer from the dance
Hail hail
Give it out
Help me out
I'm on
On the convoy
Help me on
The network
Off the convoy
Onto the network
Recognitional
Traditional
Network
Convoy one
One on one
On one
Repetition
I want a union
With a network
To recognise the
Dancer from the dance

#511
GREY CARD

My records aren't much
Like her recordings at all
Her's need a massage
Oil that heats them up
I live like a lizard
Under a rock
Most times I enjoy it
Usually the only time I
Come out from under
My warm rock
Is when someone
Rolls it off of me
I don't need oil
To heat me up
I stay warm constantly
I am sacred
Am I sacred
Sit where you want
No I wouldn't wreck
Anyone my way and
It is my natural colour
But there is nothing better
Just a different way
Of doing it

#515
IT IS MY SQUARE, THE SQUARE IS MINE

Landscaping
Land escaping
Escaping land
She's wearing glasses
And I'm supposed
To understand her
And I'd like to
Have sex with her
And I'm supposed
To understand that
Get out of here
I don't want to
Hear you talk anymore
I want to hear
Talk about you
Escaping my landscape
Like the image
On a film when
The light melts it away
It's a black
Price to pay
For something
And Someone
So beautiful
Sometimes things
Are more attractive
Left alone
Left misunderstood
More mysterious
If it's never mine
If it's always out of reach
Landscaping
Give me some space
So I can look at her
Just a little longer
Landscaping
Escaping my land

#557

AD INFINITUM

It's a new day
And I want to
Go back to sleep
In woman's tears
So I can be closer
To the ones I love
I want an aneurysm
To make things
Easier for me
I always hated
To touch bases
With something
Or someone
I don't know
Someone said
That they
Heard my name everywhere
I feel like I'm
Too popular
Here in the back
Stumbling blind
Back in the street
You say I can't
Match your pain
Why is this
All of a sudden
A competition
I'm not built
For passengers baby
And until now
I never knew what
The auteur theory meant

#547

WHEN

There is nothing
Wrong with having favourites
But this isn't
Playing favourites
When the boy's direction
Is defined as positive
And the girl's the other
I don't want to listen
To music she recognises
Into the gridlock
Projecting your voice
Through steel wool
I don't want to create
Music he recognises
I want to be my own
It's only physical
It's just physical
There is nothing
Wrong with wanting more
I see two images
Overlapped on top
Of each other
All of the time
One is a man
Drowning in water
And doing nothing
To save himself
The other is a woman
Drowning in quicksand
Struggling with all
Of her energy
To save herself
There is everything
Wrong with having favourites
When one is defined
As positive and
The other negative
How am I going to finish this
Will something ever finish this

Will anybody ever finish this
I wish I could finish this

#563
TAPESTRY TAPESTRY

A row of cabooses
And one ten year woman
Get in a line ten year woman
Get in line
He will take you down
He will knock you down
After you knock her down
I suppose you'll feel better
Is she in line now
Is she in a line
For you now
Life isn't a game of tag
You've tagged her
Now and for life
A row of cabooses
All in a line
You're like Hitler
Thinking he's an artist
You'll burn for this
I liked seeing her soft
A line isn't soft
A line is hard
You're hard
You've gotten your line
You have gotten your line
You have got in your line
Your hard
Is hateful hurtful
You took her away
Soft was fine
Beautiful
He has taken you down
I can't speak for anyone
I can't speak for anyone now
I can't be the defence
For her now
Or the prosecutor
To him now
I can't even speak

For myself now
I am in a line
Not beside myself
Behind myself
I'll go peacefully now
I won't say a word
I promise
I won't tell anyone
Ma'am
I promise
I won't tell anyone
Mister
I promise
I'm going south now
He won't let me burn him
She won't let me defend her
All this now is too much
I'll go peacefully now

A row of cabooses
Going down a track
If one derails
Put it back
To how it was
A row of cabooses
And a one ten year woman
And a ten one year man
Going down a track
If one derails
Put it back
And a boy behind himself
Put it back
Put it back
And a boy behind himself
Put it back

ESCAPE

I've erased
All of those old messages
Whether I like it or not
I changed my clothes
A long time ago
And when I saw those women
Who were either
Laying down on their backs nude
Or were mothers
Who spoke to me
"That which is inward
Must be outlawed"
Believing people who
Boarded up a temple inside of me
Was like handing a rose
To a fascist dictator
While he ignored you
But waved to the crowd

And to the ones
Who wore filters
While laying exposed
On their backs
Who never wore any colours
Natural is pleasant
Indecision is not
Are you wearing any colours?
Are you wearing your colours?
Do you know you have colours
I don't know what you want
Do you have any colours?
Do you need a warrant?
How are you doing?
Where is your smile?
All I need is to see your smile
When will you smile?
Put up a defence

Put up a defence

Open up your table
Circulation is very easy
What is your theoretical yield?
I don't want to fit the puzzle
Do you want to fit the puzzle
If you do fit
Will you still give me a smile?
The choice is your's
I won't knock you down
For making your choice
So don't knock me around
For me making mine
Do you think that the
Two lines won't touch each other?
They will if you want them to
I would still hold you up
If you gave me a smile

#363

INTO HELL'S KITCHEN

I'm cooking up
A storm with
People's minds
And it's mostly
Balls mad nasty
Fry it up
A little
Turn it down
A lot
Quickly
So I don't burn
Just scorch
Scar
You will remember me
Someone will
Remind you
That you were
Once tangled up
In my kitchen
I was told
I put people
Through hell
Cooked from raw
All the way to
Slightly scorched
Fried rotten
I am it is truth
Because because
Because because
You cooked me
Long ago
And
My recipe has
Fried me rotten
As well as you

#334

PREY

Every time I listen
To your power

I need my
Stomach pumped
Your stare
Makes my
Gums bleed
I don't need
You
You
Just think
I
Do
Do
I
Really
No
Not
At all
You prey
On my fear
Not worrying
About my
Breaking point
Prey
Pray
To your god
That when
I break
I don't break
You
With
Me

#559

THE POCKET GOD

Have you got
Your spoonful
After you ate
Your crackers
That soaked up
What little moisture
Was in your mouth
Maybe I hear
The city's voice calling
I just want to say
I don't care about you
And you always say that
You'll come
But you never do
So I'll make
My own bed
By myself
Do you do the same
I'm writing
Right now
With my book
Wide open
You think you're strong
But you don't know
That you are another Titanic
But everyone around you knows
That you are another Titanic
Just waiting to sink
Kneeling over your throne
Open wide
You aren't smiling now
How come
You aren't smiling now
Did you lose your place
Have you lost your pace
It's so easy to do
In your state
Your mouth is so dry
And you can't stop shaking

And you're deaf
To all of the voices
In the city
You've disappeared
I want to weep for you
But my eyes
Are as dry
As your mouth
And your smile are
I want to end all of this
But it's not
In my hands
It never was
It's all in your hands
And they are
Shaking so much

#239

MORPHINE

Bloodied blood fall
On desperate hands
Don't try it again
Or you'll fall in token lands

#416
TECHNIQUE

I don't want
To be a yell
I know what
I want to be
I want to be
The whisper in the dark
That you can't figure
Where it's coming from
Listening to the stories
It speaks of
Whether you like it
Or not
You want it to stop
But you can't make it
And neither can I
And neither can I

#396

INDECISION

We are everywhere at once
Where are they hiding
One of us is in you at all times
Never can you see us though
We hover over you to get a different perspective
What is going to crash on my head
We make noises in the dark
Something woke me suddenly
The heat you feel is our breath
Why am I sweating so much
All of or one of us makes
I don't dare do it
You change your mind suddenly
What was I thinking
Well, it only really takes one of us
I won't do it
But more of us increases the torture
I can't do it

#469

SUM CHANGE

A dial tone
For a custom
Made sheep
Crab war
With too many
Of us with
Panic depression
But I pulled a
Staple out of my shoe
While the silt
Was still in my mind
I saw in a pamphlet
Half of the earth
Torn off
While a dollar was
Left whole
I think she
Called them "lucky strikes"
I never was sure
The sun shone
Down on me
Even though
I wrote this
In a park
Down town
While it was
Raining
I wanted to
Steal a red rock
But I was scared
I would get
Caught
You know how
Postmen are
So I distracted
Myself by looking
At the pretty
Women smoking
In their bright

New ugly cars
That looked like
Some bug out of
A dark cellar
In a science
Fiction writer's
Fiction writer
I guess that's
What I am
Sometimes
The sum of this is
I was tempted
To steal the
Red rock again
With the crab
War torn off
And it raining
And me raining
To get caught in
I'm not sure
What this all
Means, but I
Do know that
I'm glad I'm done

#536

SCRAMBLED

The smell of after-shave
Stings my ears
How's the balance
When I'm walking
On my own hands
On my own
This song doesn't ever
Happen to me
Really I'll play with you
Listen to the music
And do that free form thing
Why am I getting
Older anyways?
Those blue and red and yellow lights
Make my ears ring
Yes, I meant to write
This this way
I don't know
If you ask me
I think it has a
Happy ending
And that's the truth
Tar and feathers
Tar and feathers
All falling out
The feedback makes
My nostrils turn in on themselves
I'm not writing
To get attention
I'm turning in on myself
Take my body and energy
Even though you don't like talking
I'll give it to you
Of my own free will
You don't like talking
But maybe you like listening
I like talking and listening
Maybe we could
Make a compromise

And just write to each other
Write on loose leaf paper
In my apartment
With only one small lamp on
Or on paper napkins
In a restaurant
Laughing quietly to ourselves
At how witty we are
Oh, but my senses
Are all scrambled up
And I think you'd
Get scared away by my
Movie-scene-like dreams
How's that for balance
And what's that fish doing
Swimming in behind
That glass?
Watching me with
Blue glassy eyes
It knows more than
I could ever hope to know
I want to go swimming
With you and
Not have to worry about
What I'm wearing
Or what's on my arms and back
I want to go swimming
With you and
The fish with the bright eyes
This is page two
Of a one page story
Stay a moment please
Talk to me
Shake my hand
And make sense
Out of my scrambled senses
With me and
Watch something
That's almost as
Graceful as you are
When you talk
I wish I knew

As much as you
But the music and my age
And my hands
With my own footprints
On both sides
Makes my writing
And my language
Interrupt all my senses
All my senses
All my senses
Want to try
And convince you (not yell at you)
That you have so much more
To offer than not talking
I'm doing my homework
Wishing you were here
Watching me with
Your special eyes
You could be my tutor
And tell me what you know
And I will listen
And nod in awe
At how beautiful you are
When you're learning something new
And passing it on to me
And it all impresses
Onto me how
Organised and how
Everything just seems
To fall into place
Whether it's good or bad
I'm not sure
I try to go on but
It's like holding
Two pens and one of them
Has no ink in it
And the other one is running low
I wish I had a bit more confidence
Then maybe I could slow down a bit
And you may be able to understand me or
Stop me if you think this is too much
Or if I've gotten off topic

Or if I'm too organised
Stop me if you want me
To slow down
So you can tell me
That it's alright
You see now what I'm getting at
What I'm getting at
What I'm getting at
You see now what I'm getting at
What I'm getting at
What I'm getting at
It's all smoothing out
It's all smoothing out
I still think
After all these years
That happy endings
Do exist somewhere
Like in the far corners
And nooks and crannies
Of my mind
Hiding there
Waiting to jump out
When my confidence is low
It's like those
Happy endings just
Jump out at me
So I have something
To hold onto for a little while longer
It sure is mentally draining
Waiting to die
Who needs execution
When the time is
Doing a far better job
Than any poison or
Electricity or rope or gun
Could ever hope to do
My pens are all running low
And my head hurts from
My happy endings
Jumping around all of the time
I'm not sure if that
Fish I watched swimming last night

Could help me now
Or if you with
All of your soft and gentle
Beauty could help me
Last night or now
Because it's like I've just
Talked to you twice
And already I'm home alone
And you wrapped up in
One of my happy endings
Jumps out from its hiding place
My balance is thrown
Way off again
And my senses are scattered
Running off in all sorts of directions
Like what rabbits do when
They see a predator nearby
Coming in faster than a chinook
Closing the gap between
Him and them in seconds
Like rabbits my senses
Usually escape unharmed
But I'm left disoriented
Panting hard with my heart racing
Nerves all taut
Because there still could
Be danger nearby
I mean you never know now a days
With the way things are now a days
With all that junk in the air
And me getting older by the half second
And getting so tired of flinching
Everyday of my life I flinch
Flinching at feelings, at people, at myself
There is no difference
Between real feelings and
Unreal feelings
Especially to the person
Who is feeling those
Real or unreal feelings
All my senses getting scrambled
Unscrambled, scrambled

Unscrambled again
And back to being scrambled
Like some sort of pendulum
Back and forth
Back and forth
I always used to pride
Myself in my senses
I guess I still do in some ways
In some ways my senses
Repulse me but
Most ways they please me
I always celebrate in my open senses
Nothing like celebrating something
You know nothing about, eh?

#564

IMBRUE

I've never known
What a
Love hate
Relationship
Means or is
Superstitions
Superstitious
Can you feel better
And worses
At the same time
Can you feel better
And worse
At the same time
Discipline is not
The enemy of
Enthusiasm
The responsibility
Is yours
It's not just
About those
Test scores
You will be locked out
Work for
What you want
Don't waste your time
Welcome
To the new
Don't try to con
A con-man
It's time
To get involved
Have you lost your faith
Did you lose your place
How strong is your base
I feel the same
Way this morning
As I did
Last night
Right or wrong

I'm going on

#571
TIDE BREAKER

The strength
That fills my eyes
Tribal rights
Of some creature
That snarls and runs
Around in circles
Inside of my stomach
Telling me that
It doesn't want food
And neither do I
Telling me that
Something nasty
Is being stirred up
By my actions
And I'm sweating
Because of my cynicism
I sweat so much
Mosquitos keep away
From me and my eulogy
I was looking at my hands
And thinking at how much
I've used them
For so many different reasons
On so many different occasions
That they should be
Scarred more than
They already are
I'm in the way
Of a river
Of collective guilt
Wondering if I have
A deficiency of
Foresight or discernment
Or if I'm chock-full
Of self assessment
Over assessment
Take it as I am
And move on
Just make sure

I leave a sample
Of my hand-written epitaph
For others to see
What feeds me
What keeps me alive
What keeps me moving
I need more
Than a hope for
Worldwide love
Or that one word changed
Changes the paragraph
Changes the whole book
These sorts of patterns
Are built on a
House of cards
One that starts to shake
When my pen
Moves across my paper
I'm afraid to see
What will happen
To that house
When it comes in contact
With winds from a
Direction different than
Love or hope
I just don't see the point
In making the effort
To find one word
That will change
A book for others
When I can write
A whole book for myself
To change myself
I believe in love
I believe in hope
That's the truth
My difference is that
My hands guide me through
The tunnel vision
Of the searchers of that one word
And all of the
Cards that are falling

Falling around me
I'm taking it as I am
And I'm moving on
And I'm making sure
That my hands
Hold the change in myself
Up to myself
And above the ones
Who search for one word
Amongst the cards
Scattered on the floor

#560

STANDING ON A STAGE

Stand aside and
Walk around me
Throw your questions
Away from me
Teaching me the strings
At school
I'm too pretty for you
When are you
Doing anything right
Get closer
Get closer to me
And stand aside
And maybe
I'll vote for you
This all fits together
The pieces are big
And they all fall into place
Like a child's puzzle
One and two and three
Slide right in
On each other
And I think
I'd like you
To put me up higher
In front of them all
But I'm scared
That my land
Is far too flat
And what's mine
Won't be
After the stage hand
Has cleaned up
All of the ticker tape
From the ash covered floor
Where people
Stood staring
With blank faces
Blank eyes
And blank thoughts

Inhaling
Exhaling
Then dropping it all
Crushing it with the
Sole of their shoe
Turning
Pivoting
Grinding the butt
Into the floor
Until it's fully put out
Hello
Hello
Am I saying something
I am saying something
Are you hearing it
You are hearing it
Then blowing the last
Of the smoke out
Uncrossing their crossed arms
Turning around
And walking way
Do I say goodbye now
Keep it up
And I'll never know
What I missed
Even when it's gone
I intentionally
Came in the back door
Because I felt uncomfortable
About coming in the front
Looking back on that track
Doing it my way
Thinking that the crowd
That the crowd that was in front of me
Like effigies waiting
To be burned
Should have been inside
Of a comic book
One that I read
In the rain
Letting the ink run
On my hands

And then dropping it all
In the gutter
Waving
Turning
Away and
Turning around
And walking away
Not bothering to watch
It all float away
Do I say goodbye now?
Yes, yes I do

www.ingramcontent.com/pod-product-compliance
Lightning Source LLC
Chambersburg PA
CBHW020658300426
44112CB00007B/429